for my mother, for being in-between,
for breaking the cycle

Published by Stanchion Books, LLC

StanchionZine.com

Edited by Katie Schmeling

Cover art by Jeff Bogle

ISBN: 979-8-88862-260-5

it skips a generation
poems from pre-internment, onward

Alison Lubar

TABLE OF CONTENTS

Superior(ity) Complex(ion)
Oakland CA, 2009

Auntie says. "Jack was handsome
to European girls, but among us,
he was a dime a dozen." He shrinks
each year. Turns to prune. Refuses
to return my mother's letters. Then
loses each of us as a spring branch
snipped before its buds unfurl. Like
so many losses of names overseas.
Whole cities. At least two. And here,
three years of camps. When Auntie
says, "I'm glad they lost the war,"
she means that no one wins when
families disintegrate into poverty, or
into mere atoms. Auntie says, "The good
die young. That's why I've made it
to my eighties."

Pancakes with Ojisan
Somewhere Pennsylvania, 1993

I slide down the tiny blue-plastic desk chair
and risk the static, shrinking into my seat
as Mrs. Wilson announces
        "Pancake breakfast with grandparents!"
And I think first,
        No one looks like Oji.
And I think second,
        I only have one person to bring.
And that day, I do.

My blue eyed, curly-haired
Bonnema [her ashes interred
under Belgian sky, in sun-warmed
concrete, topping a hill of wild perennials]
would have joined willingly,
in raspberry velour jogging suit
and mink coat. And I'm here
[with her worse half] wishing
Oji whiter.

I knew that as soon as they discovered
I have no *grandpa*, *pop-pop*, or *poppy*,
the ["classroom flirt"] boys draw up
the corners of their eyes
with middle fingers: I am
no longer mere brunette,
summer-darkened, but
reborn as "other."

I could blend in until now. [This family betrayal
is not the first.] I use my index finger and thumb
to widen my eyes, top to bottom, and stick my tongue out
at the same boys, and almost receive a principal's office referral.

[Six months later, no one eats mom's yakitori
at the classroom cultural celebration, either.]

Only twenty years after do I think of how
Oji must have felt a familiar othering, a routine
gauntlet of gazes. The other kids' third-grade
*Grand*parents probably would have made
the same, stupid face, and would have also
not gotten in any trouble.

That day, we sat in silence, mutilating
pancakes with white-plastic fork-sides
[since knives are dangerous]. Each syrupy bite,
drenched in maple-imposter, reminds me
that nothing is ever [special and] different
in a good way.

The King of Horses
Edison NJ, 2013

Horsebites never bruise. Your index and middle finger
curl to fangs, knuckles turn into the mandible of the beast
little girls never think their ponies will grow up to be,
or Black Beauty, who lost use of a limb and then his life,
useless because there's no majesty in standing with a crutch.

The horsebites from Ojisan were nothing
compared to what other little girls might have suffered
from a long line of lost pride and a grasping for power.

I never saw you in hospice, at the veteran's hospital,
in a British suit and beret, cigar, and nothing to note
you're Japanese except your eyes and skin and nails,
nothing to belie the ancestral line of samurai. I can't
imagine you any smaller, as you must have been,
eighteen years ago when I was ten, was the last time
I saw you. You filled out the plastic lawn chair,
yellow plaid woven seat and back around
the hollow aluminum frame.

You'd sit in my parents' driveway, like a king,
afraid of owning anything yourself. The apartment
you shared with Bonnema temporary enough to let you
think of leaving, but you went from nothing special
among girls to exotic and dark, handsome and dashing,
"The Oriental Fred Astaire" they called you.
And I'm still exotic, too, and so lucky, too, to seem
so foreign and dangerous and willing to bite.

MoonShine
Tacoma WA, 1930

Jack's face shimmers
                    veil of cold sweat over
the vat of moonshine,
nose scrunched   like the noble folk-
                                                  tale rabbit.
He puffs up, ruffles
                    small muscles in a white
undershirt to stand in front
of his mother, little sister, little
brother. He is thrown across the room
          again.   The rabbit throws
                                                  himself into the fire.

He decides to become a bear.   The rabbit becomes
                                                  the moon.
It's called a shiner, a black eye.   Every night,
the same pagcant. Every night,   the rabbit appears
                    less and less.

Art Imitates Life
Antwerp & Edison, 1932-1992

Here's the difference– the opalescent bowl
lives at the country house, atop a smaller mantle
than the main Antwerp address. Her husband would
spend a childhood picking strawberries instead of
painting them. Sweat shimmering on an upper lip,
sunburned cheeks just as red.

The towels in my grandparents' bathroom
were the same color as the tile, walls, tub,
pink and acidic, phosphorescent frosted glass lamps
and my grandfather's dark back awaiting a boar-bristle brushing.
In the cluttered back room, two twins made an uncomfortable king.
Visiting, at six, with my mother, I'd roll to the middle rift
to get closer after I'd struggle through Dr. Seuss. Now, I imagine
my own mother at seven, rolling into the soft, white arms
of her own. In the morning, learning to paint freckles on fruit,
smoothing over all blemishes, all the brown, rotting bruises.

Derivative Curriculum
Public School PA, 2001

"Of course we teach essential texts" he lies
to my mother and father on back-to-school night.
Because the curriculum is easy and scripted already
and not much has happened since. At least
many of us fail to make a change in economy,
liberty. Who has those taken away?
My calculus teacher pulls back
the corners of his eyes to tell a joke,
to reel us in. I feign ineptitude, fail tests.
The principal swears this couldn't have happened
because everybody loves him. In first grade I make a list
of people I hate and my teacher calls my parents. I try to be
unlikeable. I come home to declare, "I am not
a sheep," to be the one to separate myself,
claim "the other." All the while, the shame
sticks in my throat like a salmon swimming
upstream, before it's clubbed out of the water. We
never read *Farewell to Manzanar*, I still can't measure
limits at infinity, and I continue to add their names.

Only Bonnema
Edison NJ, 1996

is missing
in this apartment. Ancient make-
up spread across the low bureau
for a makeshift vanity. I only use
cakey blue and stodgy red. (Once,
I filled in a whole coloring book
with just spring-sky eyelids and
macintosh apple pouts.) I accompany
my mom to the Asian market with a full
face of paint. Today, she doesn't wipe it off.
I get a whole tub of lychee jellies. I ask for
a new tea set. (I test my mother's grief.)
It comes in a painted cardboard box
with fuschia polyester lining. I never
use it, and the jellies sit on top of the fridge
three years past expiration. Soon there is
nothing left in the freezer that's hers, either.
(No summer tomato soup, no blueberry pie,
no rainy-day brioche dough.) Jack will not
go hungry because he's still handsome
enough. Strangers see a sweet widower.
A parade of old world girlfriends feed
his ego, too. (They don't know to take him
to the Asian market.) My mother and I
sort sweater sets and home-sewn
wiggle dresses. (They still sit in my parents' basement closet.)
I take the makeup. (I never
use it again.) We miss her
arms the most.

Jack as Botanical Triptych
Edison NJ, 1970

One
As cerulean impressionist iris, from another
neglected schizophrenic who paints in waves
like Hokusai. Another influenced by the East
(my mother would say "Orientals"). Draped silk
spans shoulder to shoulder, mantle of grief. Just
a turning of head would fold the hollow stems
irreparably. Does it still smell like cigars? Of dark
aviators and bleached undershirts as you sit
in my parents' driveway like it's your own?
You didn't need to risk a mortgage. It's easier
to flee month to month. Uproot. We perennials
always find a way to still bloom.

Two
There must have been some trust
in staying. Raspberry bushes along
the apartment complex fence. Of course
you'd want a fruit with thorns. Though
you refused the kitchen otherwise,
you'd concoct ice cream with raspberry
syrup. It freezes with shards, even dessert
is sharp, but still delicious.

Three

Once, you were so cruel, my mother stabbed you with a salad fork.
Its prongs stuck in hard belly fat, its handle bounced like a cartoon
diving board, or popsicle stick garden-row markers in March wind.
I don't know what happened next, except, at that moment you
knew that one day you, too, would return to earth, interred.

It skips a generation
Suburban Pennsylvania, 2015

I'm home for a funeral and sift through photographs.
The plastic tub with the warning that people could
suffocate if you seal them in with the lid, filled
with images of my mother as a child and her mother,

and Jack. I still want to call him Oji but showing
that I know he's in me and in my own cruelty
is a cruelty I can't show to my mother, who
suffered the most under him.

I hear tales of his handsomeness from his sister,
from his girlfriend (though we never call her that),
and he seems so harmless in the pictures from the beach.

Handsome is never harmless. My mother, a toddler,
maybe older, holding a plastic shovel. Everything is grey,
but I imagine the red swimsuit and bluegreen sea. I flip through.
Striped swimsuits and smiling. He couldn't have been that mean.

And then I see, second to last, my mother's four-year-old face
frozen in terror in her backward glance at Jack. I shouldn't want
anyone to look at me like that. But I know I inherit it all.

Inedible
Suburban PA, 1991

When he throws boots, snaps rubber bands,
and horse-bites (knuckles turned to teeth) she wields
a snappy plastic-bottomed slipper. We all have

matching bunny slippers, Bonnema, my mother,
and me. Polyester wooly faces with a little pink
triangle nose. Thirteen years after her death,

I dreamt once of her on the other side of the screen
door, sitting. She couldn't talk. She lifts a hand, blue-
veined like underground rivulets, translucent blue

like eyes. I am so brown next to her, before my mother
warns me not to get too dark, to look like I don't belong
this brown. She thinks phenotype is fate, genetic destiny.

The world won't ever really change, so best to water
it down, best to dilute even if all that's left is muddy.
Rinsing brushes after an acrylic masterpiece. Elizabeth Taylor

had violet eyes. I scan pages of the American Girl Dolls
and none look like me, really. I dream of red mermaid hair,
comb mine with a fork, hoping for this utensil's alchemy. I could

use a knife instead. Mom buys me a tiger's eye bracelet
in Las Vegas from a street vendor, the chakras are really
glass beads coated in plastic, but the tiger's eye is real.

Brown, warm, striated, really gold. I used to describe
my eyes as amber in chatrooms. ASL? Also muddy.
I'd prefer that to the consumable chocolate. Explaining

any part of the body that way implies that everything
is consumable. Cannibal vision. Jack was just turning
my softness to steel, something untouchable and sharp.

Trompe L'oeil, le Cœur
Bethlehem PA, 1993

I always think the rice is ice cream,
double take at the perfect scoops
in a silver bowl. It might be a vase.
I am not completely disappointed.
When I'm warned I might not like some-
thing I trick myself to trick them. Yes, jelly-
fish is a noodle from the sea. Broccoli is
my favorite part of this. I learn to be
unexpected. I let Oji
drop the fish cheek
on my plate but let a squirm
escape at the sight of the next
delicacy, the eyeball. He teases
but not to be cruel
this time. Love is
saving the best
parts for someone
else. Even when
it looks like some-
thing else.

Catch and Release
Suburban PA, 1992

On Mother's Day, dad takes Oji fishing,
to leave us three at home. You can tell the Flemish
by our chins, strong jaw and a little bump
like a nub of brioche. In the photo from this day,
we all half-smile, my sharp-cut preschool bangs.
I'm grateful I was spared the bowl-cut. What else
is there to do but create? We roll out the pale,
chilled dough, the edges flare in small crags.
They let me use the little zig-zag wheel to cut
diamonds. I know this is kind and patient
and my precision is the best I can do. It feels a shame
to discard the edges so they let me shape them
into little cat faces. One dollop of apricot jam,
fold the edges to hug it in. As we wait for the click
of the oven to preheat the garage door rumbles.
A whole styrofoam cooler of perch tumbles
into the sink, ice slides over green bodies. It doesn't smell
like death yet. Pond-bottom overbears the sweetness
of twenty minutes ago. We three wait in the dining room
for them to finish. How can I choose whose lap I climb into?
My mother defers to hers. We are all still dusted
in flour, passive and rubenesque, waiting for the kitchen
violence to cease, the blunt-edge scrape against scales
to stop, for the reward of something sweet and free.

Writing the Wrongs
Tacoma WA, 1941

Every Monday before the camps,
Jack pawns the typewriter. This cash
is for rice, greens, any fatty meat
to flavor it all. Enough for two little
siblings, a mother. Father gone
to somewhere else for work,
a relief. No use in making
moonshine now. In the mornings,
he delivers newspapers. Greyscale
propaganda, hate is a binary. Fear
turns black then ash in the stove.
Then logging. Jack would like to
write, not cut. Make the words,
not dole them out, or demolish
the towering hemlocks that may turn
to pages one day. I imagine that
the Saturday buy-back gives him
enough time to pull those stories
from the ether, or whatever hovers
over him before he is a prisoner
of an additional, different type.

Before Any Binary
Suburban PA, 1989

I know no difference between me
and the other preschool kids except
that I was taught to color in the lines.
Lips are always red, eyelids like sky.
I fill whole books with these two shades.
I use both hands to pour from a pitcher,
and know which wooden blocks support
the highest towers. I sit mostly still,
and swing my legs under the table.
Simon Says is easy. Listening is a first
access to power and safety. The best
fruit snack is the blue T-Rex. Yellow
pterodactyls taste nothing like lemons.
Nothing compares to Bonnema's blueberry pie.
She places it on the lowest shelf of the fridge
so I can sample the middle before dinner.
The lattice crust holds so much love.
Each purple pinch of honeyed middle
stains my index and thumb. No one
tells me not to. I am the guiltless culprit,
with three and a half sets of arms to run to.
Even Oji is still sweet, for at least another year.

The Real Prize Is to Know
Officer Candidate School, 1950

I will not be
the sacrifice
they ask. To jump
on the grenade, to
turn inside-out,
back popped open
like a Christmas
cracker. My spine
as prize, vertebrae
confetti. Once, one
pushes me atop
to save himself
in this practice run,
the fake grenade
an unripened pear.
This will bruise
my lowest ribs. It's not
even a punch. This fight
is not mine to have.
And besides, we don't celebrate
holidays anymore.

Before I know better,
Antwerp, 1995

I try. We go to the hotel piano bar.
The maraschino of my Shirley Temple
bobs between chipped ice. [I'd like to
drink a bottle of grenadine.] I know no
moderation. I am too young! [Who wouldn't
let a bathtub overflow with rosy bubbles?]
Or pick all of the cashews
from the silver bowl? [I leave the peanuts.]
This effusive enthusiasm is how
I learned to love. Unmitigated optimism.
I am [chubby, but] still cute. No one
can stand Jack, but I still call him Oji.
He is charged with my care
while the other adults go to a real dinner.
Wool suit, beret, cigar. I am in dusty sandals
and a floral babydoll dress, spread to the edges
of the navy leather lounge chair. [I will not
be like the others. I will tolerate each snip
and sneer.] I play dumb and let him fill the air.
It is three days since Bonnema was interred.
[She died next to him.] No horsebites tonight.
[I know better than to try to hold his hand.]

Nothing Skips a Generation
California Temporal-Diptych

    I.   1945

When the war was over,
[on paper] it wasn't over.
There, we [became dust.
Here, we] returned to dust–
America was [a home
that held no home]
left. Even the door-
[jamb was stripped. Doors]
closed, never [to open]
for work, for us. Open
[a tin, salmon in] a can.
No [one ever can]
come back.

    II.   2015

Back in the cradle of sunshine,
this state my mother and I return to, as if
it was a type of womb. [I am too much
east-coast to be patient at the grocery
when someone lingers too long
at the wall of salad mixes.] This still
isn't the place for me. [Neither is the town
where I went to school.] When I say,
"I'm going home," I mean to a person.
We return to Auntie's with little tins
of tapas, a pain d'epi from Acme,
and oranges from our neighborhood

walk. [Everyone's backyard blossoms
in citrus. They put surplus in cardboard
boxes, on the front steps, to share.] Dinner
is all snacks, all picking. Auntie lets me use
the good Belgian crystal glasses, since now
I have another college degree. [I am still not
working on a PhD, like Ishiro.] But,
when Auntie says, "You look like Jack,"
I don't take it as an insult. I respond
[with the Scottish play], "What's done
cannot be undone."

"Very cruel race."
Oakland CA, 2001

"Very cruel race," declares
an early 2000s romcom. The bumbling starlet
listens to her dashing crush, twirls
sun-colored hair. All her cuticles are chewed.
     West-Coast twilight turns the two walls of windows
       deep-ocean dark. Three generations of us sit
     underneath the newly-installed flatscreen. My mother
   brings the DVD in her luggage, to give to Auntie afterwards.
Very cruel race registers
        like an underwater sonic boom. I laugh
       on reflex. All of us nod, and understand.
Once, Auntie beat another schoolkid
   with a yellow umbrella to prevent further bullying. Cruelty
     is preventative, and it's better to let people know
     where they stand. No furtive poisoning of rice,
      no euphemistic relocation. This is before
      I come out. This self-hate, internalized,
     eats away like the stomach cancer Granny
    and her estranged husband died from. A coyote
   that chews off a leg to escape isn't cruel. The captive
   mouse that eats her pups. Fishing with a baseball bat.
  Ending a marriage over the phone line of the rehab center.
At the end, the fair heroine gets her guy. Happily ever ever.

Parable of the Tiger
Suburban PA, 1998

Jack forgot my mother was born
in the year of the tiger. When she writes
that he can't see me anymore, that horse-
bites hurt, that words can be even worse,
he cuts us off forever.
                              [No phonecalls, even
            from the veteran's hospital twenty years later.
                  She will still take his own ashes overseas,
                  so he can rest with Bonnema, and instead
                        turn his rage to her in the afterlife.]

The lined paper might as well
be marked with stripes. In long,
thin letters, cursive loops, she still
signs it with retractable claws,
"love,"

A Good Mix
Suburban PA, 2001

My mother confesses, "Granny says white babies
are like kittens." I match my parents, at least, for
being so mixed. In AP Biology, the punnet squares
show I am lucky to be heterozygous for blue eyes.
I am "a good mix," that blends in enough. I can stay
out of the sun. In Rome, they ask me for directions.
The family curse lives under a wolf, there. Grand-
daughter of the oldest brother. I must be blessed
to live un-usurped except for what might have been.
At sixteen, I read *The Bluest Eye* and dream of what
I would fix first. That year, we get two kittens from
the store in the mall. I always begged for a puppy
instead. They are from the same litter, but only share
the Platonic ideal of Cat. The orange one loves me
but the tabby pisses on my bed. It doesn't matter
who you're related to, as long as you are lovable.

white like sun / dark like marrow
Suburban New Jersey, 2022

1. chiaro(scuro)

The white sides have scrubbed this history out of us like mud
and pollen on Mr. Martin's floors. A bone china dinner plate

becomes a mirror. I am thirteen when I first see myself
in San Francisco. My first California roll at ten. My mother says

she has a hole in her heart. Every mochi unsharpens its sides–
roasted rice tea washes this wound. The only way to connect

is through what becomes part of the body. The good rice
with a cartoon rosebud on glossy woven plastic. We split

the twenty-five pound bag. I add white miso to chicken soup.
It must be cellular magic, how the stomach links to the heart.

2. (chiaro)scuro

We don't know how to build an ancestral Shinto altar. Instead,
the mantel of white firebricks only holds birthday cards
and Bonnema's silver candlesticks.

We add Jack's blackbear statue, a sign she forgives Oji. All these
too must hold ancestral magic, from both sides, enough to break
the family curse. The sun

bleaches everything else but me. I turn from anemic cherry
blossom to bronze, something closer to steel, determined
to stay just as soft as gold.

Heavenly / Harbor
1960 / 2019

                           At

Tahoe Heavenly Valley Lodge   the Newport Harbor Marriott
                 I go in first, wiggle

in tweed pencil skirt   in cutoff denim
           past blut nub-carpet, the brass bell,
                the flanking luggage racks,
           I'm eyed with gentle interest or even better,
                indifference. Outside,

      Jack   my girlfriend
           waits while I get one room key. I pass back
           through the lobby to collect my

      [Jap]   [dyke]
          partner. We return through to get to
          our room. This time, a gauntlet. When
          your presentation is safer as a
          potted philodendron. What beautiful

    [yellow peril]   [rainbow blues]
          peace lilies flank the stairs. They are
          all fake. A part, but apart. Imposter.

Fedoras in sandstone palettes   Popped-collar pastel polos
                    with hard

arms hooked around   bellies like halved plastic
translucent necks   eggs
          What threat is here?
             all of us wonder
         each in our own
            clandestine ways.

Grand Slam
Tacoma WA, 1939

Jack takes a baseball bat
to the river. August spawning season.
          The dry rocktops steam
like the belly of a monster cut open.
          Unlaces right boot, then
left, pulls them off without sitting and sets
          each woolen sock safely
inside. There is no one out sunning today.

Salmon bounce and skip
upstream, suddenly buoyant and silver.
          Across the frothing surface,
Jack wades in halfway amidst the frenzy.
          He winds up, tight as a fist,
smacks one out of midair toward the bank–
          it lands next to his shoes.
Not all hits are lucky. Not everyone is lucky.

Jack knows he's firstborn-
blessed. Extra pressure to provide as the sole
          sober near-adult. A quarry
of four; he will share with his sister. He escapes
          hunger and a beating
that night. No one is ever full. When he's bunted
          across the room, it's so
his little brother isn't. We can only break the cycles
          we know we're a part of.

He feels nothing for the fish struck out of the air
      like a perfect pitch. Stoic hit.
They never see it coming.

For the No-Nos
Tule Lake Relocation Center, 1943

To the tar-paper shacks, no
one could live there. Did they know
this was prison? Crickets begin a soprano
chorus, each sottovoce *pian piano*.
Each note as pentatonic domino
cascades over the Monte Casino
growing along the fence. Sterno
distributed monthly, each inferno
rekindles what's lost: grannie's kimono,
the house, a hundred pounds. Cyano
sky. Peace always before the volcano.
Every body is a composite of amino
acids, chemicals. Atomic eternity. No-
thing else persists. No-
minal freedom. No
destiny manifest. No-
where. Hydrogen. No
body. Bomb. No
more.

They Won't Come Out
Oakland CA, 2013

Auntie circumvents direct
questions. She turns the camps

into the mild weather today, or
a sale at the fabric shop. But

when we get an Irish coffee
or share a wine tasting she'll let the crack of light

under the doorway of memory show four students
running from the library dropping as each passes

the guard tower. Remembers the twitches and pages
flutter away up and over the barbed wire. Or school
named by number. Or the time a neighbor accused
her of stealing a golden eagle statuette. Or beating

the bully with an umbrella for the first time to prevent
a second. Or Jack, "who suffered the most" under
his father, as the oldest, emasculated, imprisoned. We sip
something fruity from Sonoma until the last dregs

dribble onto the woven cotton placemats. The next day
these dark red spots remain; they won't come out. She
didn't escape unscathed. Jack turned into a bear
with blunted horse-teeth. She, into a totem of birds,
or a dragonfly mantle hovering above the lemon tree.

Love can look like
Bethlehem PA, 1995

printed irises
on a silk scarf
from the museum
giftshop, Irish wool
berets, three cards
on my birthday, the other two
from the grandmothers
when they couldn't write anymore.
Sitting in the front seat. Offering me
the cheek and eyeball of ginger-steamed fish.
My mother take you out of our lives,
like a fish hook in a gaping, slippery mouth.

ACKNOWLEDGMENTS

"Superior(ity) Complex(ion)" and "Art Imitates Life" were first published by *Middleground Magazine*.

"Pancakes with Ojisan" was first published in the anthology *Arriving at a Shoreline* by great weather for MEDIA.

"The King of Horses" and "Trompe L'oeil, le Cœur" first appeared as a pair in *Couplet Poetry*, Issue 4.

"'Very Cruel Race.'" first appeared in *sweet euphemism* by Alison Lubar (2023, CLASH!, an imprint of Mouthfeel Press).

"A Good Mix" first appeared in *ONE ART: a journal of poetry*.

"white like sun / dark like marrow" first appeared in *Sand Hills Literary Magazine*.

"MoonShine," "Only Bonnema," and "They Won't Come Out" were first published by *White Wall Review*.

"Inedible" first appeared in *Kissing Dynamite* 47.

"Grand Slam" was first published by *Cleaver Magazine*, Issue 39.

"For the No-Nos" was first published in Moonstone Arts' *Hiroshima Day* anthology.

ABOUT THE AUTHOR

Alison Lubar teaches high school English by day and yoga by night. They are a queer, nonbinary, mixed-race femme whose life work (aside from wordsmithing) has evolved into bringing mindfulness practices, and sometimes even poetry, to young people. Their work has been nominated for both the Pushcart Prize & Best of the Net, and they're the author of three other chapbooks: *Philosophers Know Nothing About Love* (Thirty West Publishing House, 2022), *queer feast* (Bottlecap Press, 2022), and *sweet euphemism* (CLASH!, 2023).

You can find out more at **www.alisonlubar.com** or on Twitter @theoriginalison.